Leah Flax Barber

The Mirror of Simple Souls

Winter Editions, 2025

The Mirror of Simple Souls

Columbina

Columbina on the Outskirts   13
Columbina on the Outskirts   14
Prologue   15
Columbina in the Crowd   16
The Bitter Man   18
Entr'acte   20
Columbina in the Square   21
Columbina in the Square   22
Columbina and Pedrolino   23
Columbina in the Afternoon   24
Columbina in the Afternoon   25
Columbina in the Morning   27
Columbina and Pedrolino   29
Prologue   30
Columbina in the Clearing   31
Infidelity   32

Cryptomnesia

Six Months After Reading Lear   37
Song of Songs   39
Hollywood Babylon   41
My Love is Bigger Than a Cadillac   43
Walking after Watching Fritz Lang's *Metropolis*   44
Written in Winter after Mechthild von Magdeburg   46
Cordelia's No   48
After a Figurine   49
After Jayne Mansfield's Death Car   51
Dirty Boulevard   52
Meaning of Life Question   54
Notes on Antony and Cleopatra   55

Saturnalia

The Mirror of Simple Souls 63
For a Hustler 66
For an Equinox 67
For the Rejected 69
Rune 71
Reality Math 72
Inner Snow 74
Paranoia 76
Captive Song 78
School Poem 80
What the Mind Wants 82
Ballad 83
On the Day of a Pupil Dilation 85
For the End of January 87
Internet, EU 89
Hell 91
For the New Year 92

Endnote 95
Acknowledgments 97

*The Mirror
of Simple Souls*

The correct and interesting thing is not to say, "this has come from that," but "it could have come from that."

—Ludwig Wittgenstein,
"Remarks on Frazer's *Golden Bough*"

Columbina

... certainly not "Columbina"—who never existed anywhere.

—John Rudlin and Oliver Crick,
Commedia dell'arte: A Handbook for Troupes

Columbina on the Outskirts

My mind is pure

Of heart

I escape   my alias

On the back of a mule

A stiff   glittering thread running

Through it

Beyond danger

The desert being anywhere

Where nothing is

I have often been

Stolen from

Columbina on the Outskirts

The landscape doesn't change

It dreams to stay the same

Prologue

Before literature and history

There was literature

There was history

It was ghost-faced

Bridled   experience

And we lost what we misplaced

Your wet yellow lips

Your glass

Your poison

Columbina in the Crowd

The animal shine shot through

My neck   the liquid's hot

Potential   my fate

A projectile in

The fluid world

I chew like a sword

Jester   touch the knot of

A sex   an orange light

Dances   an insect by flames

The walled

City   keeps the sewage in

And I dream of

Early light   your face

Of double

Passion   nights

In the hayloft

Where I lifted

My sleeping leg   from water

And made myself   what I am

Oh   orb

I sit on a spired fence

The Bitter Man

Rabbits with shine in their eyes

Ruffle around evil

Her red face   looming

At the Italian boys

The brown river

Threads itself   the scene

What brings me   from one stage

To the next   white melon

The bitter man   with the small stool

Speaks of survival

Like a beetle   in mirage water

But I can't see   when I come

You run at me from a distance

The shape of my character starts

Not in my mind

But in my   experience

Bring my shadow   a mistress

To the   Italians

This brown water   a sign

Leaches words   oil

Fever   runs on Earth

A vehicle

A shameless fear   opens

The living

Opens the lungs up

Entr'acte

I do as much as I can

Between moments

So I don't have to change   what happens

When I start with an impulse

You   discover

Your open hand

And the action   is clear

As a flip-book

Senses dot the periphery

Of my continent

Before   like islands   we are led

To some heaviness

My mouth leaks music

You move me on a loop

Columbina in the Square

Simmering aboveground is the feeling

I was carried off   I came back

In the sound's blackest

Register   far below the trapped music

An enormous heat rises

Merely an element of that heat

I am seduced   no   persuaded

Even if I am so clothed

In descriptionless   tyranny

I'm naked when you come

A pretty water hung   mirrors hung

Stones   at the square's entrance

There were people

Not like us   they moved like gel

Around us

In an exile   their own

Columbina in the Square

That which is   scarcely

Here   in the world   is here

Columbina and Pedrolino

In open squalor

I love you ambitionless

In Egypt   Etruria

I press my drive

Around   as host

To my life

I know the extremity   entrance

I have some fear

I want some more

I feel it dry

Oblivion   in blue clothes

Changed by trouble

And sleep   it is hot

When I move away

From you

Upstream   it is Lord

Columbina in the Afternoon

Luminous foul corridor

In late paradise

I feel   the limits

Of glory   horror and orthodoxy

I'm a savant of your history

My dress   my talent for the past

This labor   is failure

Maimed with weather

White leather

I take you   senselessly

There and there   finally

Naked   what your rights are

In the stateless world

Columbina in the Afternoon

Form protects me

From extinction

Form repeats

Still   you may press down

On the old   for the new

Soon

See my shadow

Standing lengthily

Apart   at the end

Of day   time

Its sheer necrotic novelty

An uneasy frame

In ambient red

Everything I saw

I never said

People   their early beauty

Itinerancy   its edge

A looking light

All rooms   ruin

Columbina in the Morning

My ambition is a gas

Beyond me   everywhere

Posing as air

In a new

Fractured country   we are driven out by folk

Belief kills something off

In a people

I rise   out of habit

I sleep without knowing

The time   no way to pursue it

Blue porcelain   red and yellow

Fish   I eat   the sand

Between   their heads

Like saffron

In winter   meridian

The mirror of

My jester

Goes away like wine

Columbina and Pedrolino

In the river

You rinse your painted face

Repent   an insect

We cull flowers

You eat spiders   shuddering

At the crowd   I slide the light inside

If I could invent a family

Whom I belong to   again

There might only be

Water   and how little water heals

I descend with my hideous

Sister   a young voice

Moves   mesh through a curtain

Fevered we are with disgust

Being an actress   I touch your hand

Without touching it

Prologue

Somewhere from above

I tried to fit my vicious will   inside

My form

Candy-lipped mime

Book from which the books come

The books

That populate the world

The powder

That populates

Like death

The world

Columbina in the Clearing

Immanence   my sponge

In vinegar

The plot   humiliate

Then   become human

Blue reds run

Wild   in the mineral cold

Coloratura of the general

West   I feel your

Destruction

In the unpopulated   images

Infidelity

My infidelity to the Earth

A typeless beauty

In the highlands   the single

Humanoid figures   no

My compass

I love them for their natures

They have nothing   and come in alone

It is work   to be

Thought of   is to stay alive

I have already been living

At the heart   I know

I have sinned   not how

Cryptomnesia

Let him who has something to say step forward and be silent!

—Karl Kraus,
"In These Great Times"

Six Months After Reading Lear

The cause of history

A basic irrationality

Surrounded by lives

The past   a dictator   says love

A collective orgasm

In the presence of reality

The drum kicks in sadly

At the joke

I don't want to be in the ground

I want to be in the world

To protect myself from it

This is a rigid art

That sings inward

Like the shame-flower

In domesticated green

Will it all be destroyed?

Definitely

I will hear it on my radio

In the 22nd century

It will be like a snow globe inside me

Life   barbaric

And delicate   lyric

Song of Songs

Like fucking a fume

Away

This flame

And it's a future to make love

Your good ointments

Your name

A domino

In a room full of dominoes

Desirelessness

It's in the world

A little taste of surrender

Like murder

Climbing up the brown buildings

Shimmering down

On bits of ticker tape

Hollywood Babylon

Bert Brecht hated New York

But he loved Chaplin

Chaplin was blonde and short

He had two child brides

We know the end

White dress and a pair of penny loafers

Playing poker with a deck of cards

All jacks

Things are things

Ideas are also things

They all come from somewhere

On the boardwalk

There's a thief

A rose pinned to his dick

A shirt with little mirrors sewn into it

Warped little mirrors

Sewn on black velvet

My Love is Bigger Than a Cadillac

An act of self-hatred

Like butter on water

When you wear those

High-neck blouses

That make me want to see you

A woman touches Jesus

But He doesn't see her

Jesus eats crazy amounts of bread

A Kate Bush song goes

Have you ever seen a picture

In the suburbs of my love

A karaoke goes

You are beautiful

You are so beautiful

But you are not as beautiful as the beginning

Walking after Watching Fritz Lang's *Metropolis*

One way of living is mercy

A movielike beauty

Made of hand-drawn eyes

Many times you're in a place

Where you don't want to be

No one comes out of their grave

You will go your whole life

Without seeing it

Everyone   has thought of something

In the afternoon

I have made myself ugly

Exactitude is cruelty

Whim   satisfies endlessly

We are going to hell

For reading this

Before bed

Men are playing chess in the park

Fathers are notoriously hard to forgive

Chess is a great muscle

Against the

"What is the future?" question

It's hard to do just one thing

To sing exactly

What you are

In the tension of the morning

Commute   a clean sexual energy

Comes through in the details

The demonic finalist

Of material culture

Is love

There is paraphernalia of life

All over

A woman

Written in Winter after Mechthild von Magdeburg

God said

I couldn't help but be God

The romance between the maid

And the Lord

The androgynous prelapsarian body

Resurrection   because the world

Thinks of us

Second life   because it sees us

Let the mind recognize itself

In the kitchen

It will ask for nothing

Like sleep

Only a trace of it

Will remain in the body

Who made this book?

I made it   with my powerlessness

To live   lie down in snow

Cordelia's No

You don't want all my love

How much would you pay for it?

You need to feel the danger

To be influenced by everything ever

To move between absolute seduction

And confusion

I was thinking of the goddess   of course

The violence and fraud

Humiliate me in front of the government

I'll win   living

The illusion of ending is art

After a Figurine

Power walking the apartment

Taste a food with my digit

In a terrible bin

More like a strobe

What did I win?

A bag of black vinegar   this platform

Picture from the gone world

Your meaty hands

Merciless pietà

The basic shame that exists

Within us

In all arts

The brutal big effect

The brutal arts

After Jayne Mansfield's Death Car

There's money all over

What we invented

But I wouldn't weep for it

Culture precedes everything

The giant of him

A fecundity

It brings the world to its knees

To name a single thing in this picture

Big foods seduce the knife

Lay your hands on me

In thirty-eight minutes of sunset

There's no era   only a desire

To square

Square up

Dirty Boulevard

The freedom of love   it astounds me

When we walk by the furniture stores

With their waterbeds as big as houses

On the dirty boulevard

Loneliness is pitiful

Freedom is my dream   I always forget

The pornographic dream of a vista

You're gonna get what you want

You're gonna get it

And then you're gonna lose it

Like the stars   all

Uninterrupted and sweet

A website of snow

So red it stains your eye

Stains your eyes green and red

When you look away from it

Meaning of Life Question

The dialectical transparency

Of William Carlos Williams

Like coming home and

Feeling glad to be alive

Blood is red

So why do we need

Other colors?

I'm not sure what it means

That I am me

To you

To be me is something like

The meaning of life question

So little happens

Notes on Antony and Cleopatra

Medea was a pharmakon

My oblivion

Later   you will really lose

Antony   so tough

He drank horse piss

The secret   use everything

Address someone   who is not

Deep gossip   absence

All is horizon

It is unskillful to eat

Your tool

Rome   happens

When you really start

Falling apart

In aught   August

Surrender youth

Or try not to surrender it

Intrinsicate knot

A neologism for war

Begins with nay

Supersaturation

Rips you apart nightly

To create   the night

(Isis and Osiris)

As water is in water

Women's secrets

I saw the back

Of a black hole

Living here   shattered

Ultra chartreuse   Venus

That youth

It was pissed out of us

In the spring water

An ancestral urge

To taste for poison

Time is out of joint

Dripping slowly

You go there   there is talk

You go there and you talk

And that's doubt

The wounded chance

To think in public

I will follow you

The I   where the nay was

The worm will   go through

The guts

Of the beggar-king

A crooked elegy

Digested   we will give up everything

To experience each other

At the severest limits of   our lives

Out of time

In Judas's unnaturalness

And villainy

The messenger

Form   a lengthy suicide

Effacing the whole

Dream

Saturnalia

The heroes of folk humor often descend into hell.

—Mikhail Bakhtin,
Rabelais and His World

The Mirror of Simple Souls

When we sat on a slab of flat rock

I was repulsed

Until I felt you

Behind the museum

When I was lost in water   I understood

But I won't tell you

I looked at the round mirror

Affixed to the tree

The round mirror

Affixed to the tree

Reminded me

Of *The Mirror of Simple Souls*

Which I had read for class

Earlier that year

The Mirror of Simple Souls

Is about

The seven stages of annihilation

The Soul goes through

On its path to Oneness

With God through Love

The title *The Mirror of Simple Souls* implies

That a book is a mirror

It cures the soul of its complication

By manipulating its reflection

Or revealing it

A book   like a mirror

Is held to the face

Complication lies

On the surface

In the face

If language is sullied

Through use

Is this use?

Each moment of wakefulness

Is followed by delusion

To suffer means

To be acted upon

When I think of you

I want to make a picture of you

So I can keep you

A glass of milk with ice

The elegant cross

Of your arms

In a sleeveless top

The hair is love   it bothers the face

For a Hustler

There's no one born of woman

Who can tell you

I feel such a transgression

To deform a life

With the half-known

Elixir

Is everything to be confided?

We have despite our odor

Lived innocent lives

Your parquet floors

Your pubic hair

In cave light

For an Equinox

I dip my dirty hand

Into a new tub of lotion

A loss of faith seems the only way forward

Earth is more than surface

We've barely touched it

The past

It goes away constantly

Squeeze the foam

Like a wildcard

A blue joker

Out of me

It's oral

And anarchic

Nothing but hell

I want a baby

Milky vetiver

There are signs

On the mountains

And death loves

Desertion

No   survival does

It looks like death

But it isn't

When you die

Another you

Appears immediately

That's annihilation

For the Rejected

The early morning blue flame

It's like a nursery rhyme

But it rails me

I don't want to be you

Or be like you

But I want you

This is segue music   desire

Inside cryotherapy

The mind is already there

How unlucky

Beyond the pleasure principle

A razor through fat

In sotto voce

Everything is known

Specifics change

When the pantomime runs out

I want proof

From the stereo

Of sound

Your voice

Milk on sea

A game of dare and dare

Omnes   my soliloquy

Rune

I'm back with a theory

The theory coagulates

Wildly

And is young   like reason

People are used to being asked

For more

They are global with shame

In a paltry blue state

Drinking locust juice

No feeling is long for this world

Only objects are long

And even then

Reality Math

There's no beginning of the end of horror

I want love from this petroculture

Apocrypha and you   uncut

In a sweater wet with silver

Telling them nothing

In the inner life of history

It's space that is profane   not Earth

Each word is a bribe

Literal and hieroglyphic

Objects become dangerous

No   they show their danger

When the sun goes completely down

I want to see many pictures

I wonder what my life will be like

Inner Snow

Cities are where the love is

Not in this Puritan hell

But I like the wrought iron lampposts

Behind you

While you drink milky coffee not smiling

The heat of the day

The heat of the computer

A wood moth falls out of the tree

And lives an hour

I want to live

I had a dream like this   just a color

The rapid weather

Shit smell of summer

The limestone's reflection

In the black glass

I'm Scardanelli   I go mad

At the Paris keychain dangling

From your belt

At techno night

The intricacy of speed

Its vividness

Paranoia

Whisper your name into my locket

Sloped under a radiator

On the table on all flours   bleeding

The glory days are happening

In my apartment

When water runs the wrong way

Down the steam knife

The future is an open question

A festive spanking later

We will cry for an hour

Together from 8 to 9 PM

We will cry at the fact

That everyone in this video

Lived their whole lives

Captive Song

There are few things in this world I haven't seen

Pictures of

My hands   I enter

The new room

I could stand three feet on my knees

People like to read in languages

They don't speak

Then they can enjoy looking

At characters and don't have to use

Their mouths

Some people never tell anyone   anything

Their whole lives

And some never say any words at all

You are free to be the perpetrator

If you want to be

I think I understand your   inclination

I won't make you say

Any words

I won't make you read

Any books

Forget what I said

I could sleep anywhere

Standing up

School Poem

Summer used to be life

Now it's death

And winter   which used to be death

Is more like sleep

September's excitements

Its dead kinds of beginning

Where one accepts the end

I love the vernacular   but

I can't say

I don't like Latin   its punishing intelligibility

Making a farce of this age

First you get your best thought

What the Mind Wants

Origin is the goal

To want to be denied it

And worse   to be denied it

I miss my disaster

Sending me down on the dumbwaiter

Touching all the elevator buttons

In kidskin gloves

In the doorway you say

What do you have to say for yourself?

In a theater of the whatever

Life is not about happiness

Ballad

Full moon tonight

And these clouds are a dune

A 24-hour gong

The louder the better

To love   see everything as time

And time as obsession

A pain like chewing gum

In the subarctic

You chase your demon

Across the breaking ice

Will it be different

From perfection?

Death   so moral

And outsiderly

A black pomade in my hair

No   a clear red

Like an embryo

In oily glass

I am tired now from the meal

I want to touch you

With my eyes closed

Like someone learning

Not every word is saved

By its ending

On the Day of a Pupil Dilation

Everyone is only who they are

To you

At the moment they are

To you

That's who everybody is   to everyone

You can't write something and then

Be dead and reborn

My skin is intense like everyone's

The day's appearance

Had a touch of insanity

In the lucid bright

Oranges and blues

It was sinister

Weak messianism   the morning

Its cold light

I want to know myself

Because I need myself

More than I need others

Yet I needed you

Like a black ribbon

Needs throats

Or the braids of little girls

For the End of January

I guess I loved it

I didn't mean to

The real threat is daily life

After all this time   the trouble

With experience

It weighs you down

When man first walked on Earth

How much glimmer?

A bedside table

Littered with paper notes

A poet's not a radio

When I want to say something

An illogic follows

I stayed up late

I liked the café

I will show my hands

Inside the puppet

Internet, EU

Jesus   tell me

What it's like to be dead

I forget

How quickly the moment passes

To dream the life you're entering

It will be August tomorrow

I will take a picture with my mind

Syntax is time

I'd ride its motorcycle

Cold as puce

The color of Babylon

What makes you think of me?

A parody of the 20th century

In basic existence   edged

For years on end

When I hover over dead text

It becomes a link

A cash business

Selling kidneys

A person or thing that watches

Or stands as if watching

Hell

Love makes you believe in hell

You have long red hair like hell

I love you like Nicole Kidman

Hell leaves you everywhere

Hungry   desperate and dead

In a black Buick

With four   five hands

Behind your back

A Bohemia of distance

Across the tiny garnet flowers

And everything slow moving

For the New Year

A sweet little pillbox

At the end of an orgasm

In the uilleann pipes

In the boarding school in the mind

The heaven we feel

The heart's like a deity

To a horse lover

The winter light

The rarest brick towers

The world is the place

Where you hurt

Where you are

In the courtyard with cold German breakfast

It was a gorgeous day

Endnote

In the foggy origins of Carnival, the possible genesis of the *commedia dell'arte*, thinkers like James Frazer and Mikhail Bakhtin discovered echoes of the Roman festival Saturnalia. Saturnalia honored Saturn, god of seed-sowing and time, in a week-long celebration of hierarchy inversion and moral freedom. All work and business were suspended, masters waited on slaves, public gambling was permitted, and a mock king was appointed by lot to preside over the festivities.

Columbina is the young, cunning servant girl in the *commedia* stock cast. Scholars sometimes regard the anglicized "Columbina" spelling as a distortion of the original "Colombina." And so when Rudlin and Crick write "certainly not 'Columbina'—who never existed anywhere," they conjure two things: the disfavored spelling, and a sense of disappearance in the figure herself.

A source whose origin is unresolved remains inexhaustible. Saturnalia was itself origin-seeking, conjuring a mythic age of innocence and spontaneous bounty under the rule of Saturn. It was also statecraft, a social safety valve. The comedy of Saturnalia is a melancholy memory-image: the slightness, revealed in exception, of an unforeclosed possibility of liberation.

Commedia dell'arte imagery has often been revived. The eighteenth-century painter Jean-Antoine Watteau famously reanimated *commedia* tropes in the Rococo period. Of Watteau, Walter Pater wrote, "He was always a seeker after something in the world, that is there in no satisfying measure, or not at all."

Acknowledgments

"Origin is the goal" ("What the Mind Wants") and "weak messianism" ("On the Day of a Pupil Dilation") are both references to Walter Benjamin's *Theses on the Philosophy of History*. The former is a quotation from Karl Kraus appropriated by Benjamin.

The image of Earth as sacred and space as profane ("Reality Math") comes from Mircea Eliade's *The Sacred and the Profane*.

"Lie down in snow" ("Written in Winter after Mechthild von Magdeburg") is borrowed from Susan Howe's *The Europe of Trusts*. "I made it, with my powerlessness" is adapted from this passage, from von Magdeburg's *The Flowing Light of the Godhead*: "Ah! Lord God! Who has written this book? I in my weakness have written it, because I dared not to hide the gift that is in it."

"I want to know myself / Because I need myself / More than I need others" ("On the Day of a Pupil Dilation") is adapted from this passage, written by Clarice Lispector in a piece of literary criticism referencing the Copacabana Fort Revolt of 1922: "This was all the result of 1922 ... We are hungry for knowledge about ourselves because we need ourselves more than we need others."

"Deep gossip" ("Notes on Antony and Cleopatra") is a reference to Henry Abelove's book of the same name.

I am grateful to the editors at *Conjunctions*, *The Common*, and *Peach Mag*, where some of these poems have previously appeared.

My thanks to Peter Gizzi and Matvei Yankelevich. Thank you to my family: Alexander Barber, Karen Flax, and Sotirios Barber. For ideas and encouragement, thanks to Filip Marinovich, Rachel Glaser, Isabella Miller, Nellie Prior, Colin Drohan, Kai Ihns, Riley Jones, Scout Turkel, and Tom Carlson.

LEAH FLAX BARBER is a writer from Chicago. She holds an MFA in poetry from the University of Massachusetts–Amherst. Her poetry and criticism have appeared in *Conjunctions, Cleveland Review of Books, The Common, Peach Mag,* and *Reading in Translation.*

The Mirror of Simple Souls
Copyright © Leah Flax Barber, 2025

ISBN 978-1-959708-14-8
LCCN 2025930683

First Edition, 2025 — 1,000 copies

Winter Editions, Brooklyn, New York
wintereditions.net

The image on the cover is a detail of Leroux's 1686 engraving of Caterina Biancolelli in the role of Colombina.

WE books are typeset in Heldane, a renaissance-inspired serif designed by Kris Sowersby for Klim Type Foundry, and Zirkon, a contemporary gothic designed by Tobias Rechsteiner for Grilli Type. The layout and covers are done by the editor following a series design by Andrew Bourne.

This book was printed and bound in Lithuania by BALTO print with eco-friendly Munken papers. Manufactured by Arctic Paper in Sweden, Munken meets EU Ecolabel, Forest Stewardship Council, and Cradle to Cradle certification standards.

WE is grateful for the support of our subscribers, and extends special thanks to recent Supporting and Lifetime Subscribers: Anonymous, Anonymous (in memory of the Beaubiens), Yevgeniy Fiks, Elizabeth T. Gray, Jr., and Katy Lederer.

WE is a member of the Community of Literary Magazines and Presses (CLMP). Our 2025 program is supported by a Small Press Future Fund grant from CLMP and the Mellon Foundation.

 Winter Editions

Emily Simon, IN MANY WAYS

Garth Graeper, THE SKY BROKE MORE

Robert Desnos, NIGHT OF LOVELESS NIGHTS, tr. Lewis Warsh

Richard Hell, WHAT JUST HAPPENED

Marina Tëmkina & Michel Gérard, BOYS FIGHT

Claire DeVoogd, VIA

Monica McClure, THE GONE THING

Ahmad Almallah, BORDER WISDOM

Hélio Oiticica, SECRET POETICS, tr. Rebecca Kosick

Heimrad Bäcker, DOCUMENTARY POETRY, tr. Patrick Greaney

Robert Fitterman, CREVE COEUR

Karla Kelsey, TRANSCENDENTAL FACTORY: FOR MINA LOY

Alan Gilbert, THE EVERYDAY LIFE OF DESIGN

Betsy Fagin, FIRES SEEN FROM SPACE

Cristina Pérez Díaz, FROM THE FOUNDING OF THE COUNTRY

Sarah Riggs, LINES

Leah Flax Barber, THE MIRROR OF SIMPLE SOULS

Michael Kasper, START ANYWHERE

POSTCARDS OF THE SIEGE: VISUAL CULTURE DURING THE SIEGE OF LENINGRAD (1941–1944), ed. Polina Barskova

Nathalie Quintane, THE CAVALIER, tr. Jonathan Larson

Monique Wittig, THE LESBIAN BODY, tr. David LeVay

Monique Wittig, ACROSS THE ACHERON, tr. David LeVay